Stella Andromeda

ASTRO
AFFIRMATIONS

Empowering the Zodiac
for Positive Change

Hardie Grant

BOOKS

January

April

February

May

March

June

INTRODUCTION

At the beginning of the twentieth century, a French psychologist and pharmacist called Emile Coué came up with the idea of conscious autosuggestion to help overcome negative thoughts. This consisted of saying the following phrase twice a day: Every day, in every way, I'm getting better and better (Tous les jours à tous points de vue je vais de mieux en mieux). It became known as the Coué Method.

Today we think of this form of conscious autosuggestion as affirmations – statements that can help you to focus on the positive and challenge self-sabotaging thoughts. They needn't be limited to just one statement as was the case with the Coué Method. Affirmations help us counteract an insistent negative voice in our own minds that can inhibit us and prevent us from reaching our true potential. Positive affirmations are as self-fulfilling as negative ones, so it makes sense to focus on the positive. Getting into the habit of a daily affirmation can, over time, go a long way towards improving the sort of self-confidence that enables us to progress.

In *AstroAffirmations*, there are 366 daily affirmations (including 29th February for leap years) which are linked to each of the relevant 12 sun signs through which we pass during the year.

In addition, there is a birthday affirmation specifically for those born on that day, to reinforce the astrological influence of the sun sign under which they are born. But whenever we are born, we are all affected by the 'astrological weather' that shifts and shapes our daily experience and changes throughout the year. Working with this can amplify the benefit of our daily affirmation and offer guidance and focus for each and every day of the year.

THE 12 SIGNS
OF THE ZODIAC

Aries
21 MARCH–20 APRIL

Key words for those born under Aries are independent, pioneering and outgoing. Generally straightforward, sometimes to the point of bluntness, there is something childlike about Aries in their immediate enthusiasm and openness to new ideas and action. This is because Aries is the first sign of the zodiac, representing the birth of the astrological New Year. It is also a fire sign. Aries can often spark activity and motivation in others but, like fire, they need to be constantly refuelled by both new ideas and the support of others to get things done.

Whatever your sign, use this fearless energy to focus your affirmations.

Aries' opposite sign is Libra.

Taurus
21 APRIL–20 MAY

Those born under Taurus are dependable, tenacious and hardworking. For Taurus, security lies mainly in material possessions and they are not suited to a nomadic existence, preferring to put down roots and create a stable home life wherever they are. This need for security means that they are often good with money, making it and keeping it and spending it on their home, creating a secure place for themselves and their beautiful purchases. Taurus likes to feel contained and is very self-contained in many ways, to the point of appearing reserved and keeping their feelings private.

Use this period of Taurus influence to focus on what really matters to you and work to stay grounded in your affirmations.

Taurus' opposite sign is Scorpio.

THE 12 SIGNS
OF THE ZODIAC

Gemini
21 MAY–20 JUNE

Gemini are airy, communicative, versatile, energetic in mind and adaptable by nature. There's something quixotic about them, which fascinates others. Occasionally rather lax about the truth of a situation, this is less about deliberately lying than skirting around the issue when it suits them. Considered rather capricious as a consequence, there is a duality to Gemini's make-up, which is depicted in the sign's representation by the mythological twins Castor and Pollux, who were born of the same mother but two different fathers. This duality can be seen in an ability to assume two (or even more) roles, which is made possible by an easy adaptability as Gemini is a mutable sign. This can also make Geminis restless, seeing them flit from one idea, or job, to another – a sort of hyperactivity that can result in a dissipation of energy.

Use Gemini energy to inspire you but remember to come down to earth to actually make it happen.

Gemini's opposite sign is Sagittarius.

Cancer
21 JUNE–21 JULY

Loyal, kind, sympathetic – all this is true of Cancer, but they can also appear a little 'crabby', contradicting what people think they know about them because, like the crab, there is a very gentle and soft interior that occasionally needs quite a hard exterior to hide and safeguard their feelings.

Cancer is ruled by the mysterious, constantly waxing and waning Moon, which tends to summon our more feminine, intuitive side. Whatever your sign, during the zodiac period of Cancerian influence, there's much to be gained from reflecting on things, just as the moon reflects the sun's light, to help focus your affirmations.

Cancer's opposite sign is Capricorn.

♌

Leo

22 JULY–21 AUGUST

Leos like to shine in their world, radiating energy and exuding cheerfulness like a sunny day. That energy often makes them strongly creative, whether in artistic or business endeavours, and even with an eye to their own legacy, sometimes to the extent of wanting to be immortalised in some way through their creation of something of lasting value.

Their view of life is generally optimistic, and this often makes them extremely generous and straightforward, magnanimous in attitude and willing to share their own good fortune. It's partly this that makes them successful. It's a good time to shine a light on our dreams and aspirations, helping our confidence to soar and taking pride in our accomplishments.

Leo's opposite sign is Aquarius.

♍

Virgo

22 AUGUST–21 SEPTEMBER

Traditionally represented by the virgin (or chaste corn maiden), there is something of a paradox about Virgo because this sign is also linked to the creative and fertile Earth Mother, so we could say Virgo is all about abundance, but an abundance that is often kept in check. Practical but discriminating, conscientious but warm, adaptable but reserved, they are a unique combination of opposites that can sometimes clash and cause them stress.

Ruled by Mercury, planet of communication, in Virgo this can sometimes be expressed through a critical eye cast on ourselves and others. With a tendency towards self-sufficiency, during Virgo weather it's important to remember the benefit of harmonious relationships and utilise our powers of observation for the good of these, sometimes keeping our own counsel.

Virgo's opposite sign is Pisces.

THE 12 SIGNS
OF THE ZODIAC

♎ Libra
22 SEPTEMBER–21 OCTOBER

Key words for Libra are balance, harmony and diplomacy. Generally inclined to creating peace, using silver-tongued words to soothe and placate, they are also good listeners and the least argumentative sign of the zodiac. That doesn't mean Libra doesn't enjoy debating issues; in fact, they relish it, weighing up the pros and cons of a situation and trying to balance both sides according to their astrological sign, the scales. There's a huge sense of fairness which drives them and also an objectivity that allows Librans to see both sides.

Ruled by the planet Venus, the planet of love with its emphasis on beauty, art and pleasure, there's an inclination towards luxury and loveliness, and Libra also emphasises what's democratic and fair. During Libra weather, there's an opportunity to look at what might be out of balance in our lives, and how to work with its influence to recreate the harmony that can free us to enjoy life more fully.

Libra's opposite sign is Aries.

♏ Scorpio
22 OCTOBER–21 NOVEMBER

Scorpio is considered one of the most powerful (and occasionally difficult) signs: a real poker player, there's just so much going on inside that's not always obvious to those around them. They also need solitude to process all that internal activity and this occasional need to withdraw can give them a reputation for being moody. Another facet of Scorpio that's not always easily understood is their idealism. They actually believe in the best and can be very positive about life. This also stems from a sense of regeneration, that anything can be improved upon or made anew.

Ruled by both Pluto, planet of the underworld, and Mars and depicted by the scorpion with a sting in its tail, there's an intensity about Scorpio weather that can help us connect to our innermost desires or shed old preoccupations and inhibitions that restrict us. This is powerful energy, but don't fear it because it could be transformational.

Scorpio's opposite sign is Taurus.

Sagittarius
22 NOVEMBER–21 DECEMBER

Sagittarius is all about independence of mind, body and spirit, and this lies at the heart of their approach to life. Positivity radiates from them because in Sagittarius' world, anything and everything is possible: they are seriously optimistic about life and somehow this seems to open doors for them, not least because their positivity is hard to resist. All this makes them very attractive to be around, but the downside is that they may not be around for long. This independence of spirit can make Sagittarius very restless, always in pursuit of new ideas, places and people.

Ruled by the benevolent planet Jupiter, there's something optimistic about Sagittarius weather. We may not know where it takes us, but when the centaur fires its arrow we can follow its trajectory with an open heart and mind, and this is the benefit of Sagittarian weather for us all.

Sagittarius' opposite sign is Gemini.

Capricorn
22 DECEMBER–20 JANUARY

Capricorn is depicted as a sure-footed, nimble goat, inspired to reach the mountain top and happy to do this through graft and application. This isn't about the easy route to status and acclaim in life, but how we work to achieve our ambitions and what we want through our own efforts rather than through luck or chance.

Ruled by the planet Saturn, often referred to as the taskmaster of the skies, there are no shortcuts to success during Capricorn weather, but with self-sufficiency and commitment, there's every possibility of success. There's also a practical and playful aspect to Capricorn which means that we can approach what we must do with optimism, knowing that we can work out what we need to do to achieve our goal, even if it's not immediately obvious.

Capricorn's opposite sign is Cancer.

THE 12 SIGNS
OF THE ZODIAC

Aquarius
21 JANUARY–19 FEBRUARY

There's a humanitarian streak at the heart of Aquarius that embraces friendship groups and acquaintances of all races, colours and creeds, and also has the vision and ideas that can benefit mankind. This is less about immediate gratification than about how we can work together in the long term for the greater good of the many rather than the individual.

Aquarius is ruled by the planet Uranus, a disruptive but beneficial influence, shaking up the order of things to create opportunity for change, innovation and invention. Aquarius weather gives us the opportunity to examine the status quo and check out whether it's in the best interests of the majority. Use Aquarius weather to refresh your ideas, focusing on positive change that will liberate you from old, restrictive ideas that no longer serve you.

Aquarius' opposite sign is Leo.

Pisces
20 FEBRUARY–20 MARCH

Imaginative, empathic, intuitive and sometimes spiritual to the point of being mystical, Pisces has a quicksilver mind, like fish catching the light as they dart through the watery depths. This, the twelfth astrological sign of the zodiac, is all about the deep spiritual regeneration that heralds the new (as embodied in the sign that follows, Aries). And as a water sign, Pisces links the two worlds of internal and external life, existing at a point on the cusp of reality and in the realms of imagination, making them one of the most naturally creative of the signs.

Ruled by the planet Neptune, god of the sea, we can immediately see that Pisces has hidden depths. Here lies great scope for imagination but also for compassion, for ourselves and others. Pisces weather is a wonderful opportunity to listen to that still, small voice within and see what it might reveal about our hopes, aspirations and dreams.

Pisces' opposite sign is Virgo.

THE 12 HOUSES

The birth chart is divided into 12 houses, which represent separate areas and functions of your life. When you are told you have something in a specific house – for example, Libra (balance) in the fifth house (creativity and sex) – it creates a way of interpreting the influences that can arise and are particular to how you might approach an aspect of your life.

Each house relates to a sun sign, and in this way each is represented by some of the characteristics of that sign, which is said to be its natural ruler. Three of these houses are considered to be mystical, relating to our interior, psychic world: the fourth (home), eighth (death and regeneration) and twelfth (secrets).

1ST HOUSE
THE SELF RULED BY ARIES

This house symbolises the self: you, who you are and how you represent yourself, your likes, dislikes and approach to life. It also represents how you see yourself and what you want in life.

2ND HOUSE
POSSESSIONS RULED BY TAURUS

The second house symbolises your possessions, what you own, including money; how you earn or acquire your income; and your material security and the physical things you take with you as you move through life.

3RD HOUSE
COMMUNICATION RULED BY GEMINI

This house is about communication and mental attitude, primarily how you express yourself. It's also about how you function within your family, and how you travel to school or work, and includes how you think, speak, write and learn.

4TH HOUSE
HOME RULED BY CANCER

This house is about your roots and your home or homes, present, past and future, so it includes both your childhood and current domestic set-up. It's also about what home and security represents to you.

5TH HOUSE
CREATIVITY RULED BY LEO

Billed as the house of creativity and play, this also includes sex, and relates to the creative urge and the libido. It's also about speculation in finance and love, games, fun and affection: affairs of the heart.

6TH HOUSE
HEALTH RULED BY VIRGO

This house is related to health: our own physical and emotional health, and how robust it is; but also that of those we care for, look after or provide support to – from family members to work colleagues.

7TH HOUSE
PARTNERSHIPS RULED BY LIBRA

The opposite of the first house, this reflects shared goals and intimate partnerships, our choice of life partner and how successful our relationships might be. It also reflects partnerships and adversaries in our professional world.

8TH HOUSE
REGENERATION RULED BY SCORPIO

For death, read regeneration or spiritual transformation; this house also reflects legacies and what you inherit after a death, in personality traits or materially. And because regeneration requires sex, it's also about sex and sexual emotions.

9TH HOUSE
TRAVEL RULED BY SAGITTARIUS

The house of long-distance travel and exploration, this is also about the broadening of the mind that travel can bring, and how that might express itself. It also reflects the sending out of ideas, which can come about from literary effort or publication.

10TH HOUSE
ASPIRATIONS RULED BY CAPRICORN

This represents our aspiration and status, how we'd like to be elevated in public standing (or not), our ambitions, image and what we'd like to attain in life, through our own efforts.

11TH HOUSE
FRIENDSHIPS RULED BY AQUARIUS

The eleventh house is about friendship groups and acquaintances, vision and ideas, and is less about immediate gratification than about longer-term dreams and how these might be realised through our ability to work harmoniously with others.

12TH HOUSE
SECRETS RULED BY PISCES

Considered the most spiritual house, this is also the house of the unconscious, of secrets and of what might lie hidden, the metaphorical skeleton in the closet. It also reflects the secret ways we might self-sabotage or imprison our own efforts by not exploring them.

Daily Affirmation

Those things that look as if they are falling apart may actually be falling into place.

JANUARY

What holds you back isn't what you are, but what you think you're not.

Birthday Affirmation

Daily Affirmation

Joining the crowd is easy, standing alone
and doing the right thing is hard.

JANUARY

02

Consciously choose those friends that you
know will have your back.

Birthday Affirmation

Daily Affirmation

Each day, face something that scares you and do it anyway.

JANUARY

03

Hold fast to your dreams, they are the beginnings of positive change.

Birthday Affirmation

Daily Affirmation

No dream can work unless you're prepared
to do the graft.

JANUARY

When one door closes,
find another to open.

Birthday Affirmation

CAPRICORN   19

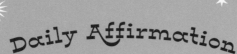

Daily Affirmation

There is only one secret when it comes
to getting ahead and that is to get started.

JANUARY

05

Sometimes passion just needs a little
courage to make it happen.

Birthday Affirmation

There's no point dwelling on yesterday,
each day is a new beginning.

JANUARY

Hold on to your vision and trust it will unfold
at the right time and in the right way.

Birthday Affirmation

Daily Affirmation

A glass is neither half-empty nor half-full
but always refillable.

JANUARY

07

You are what you repeatedly do,
so choose your efforts wisely.

Birthday Affirmation

Daily Affirmation

Smart people know they can learn from everything and everyone.

JANUARY

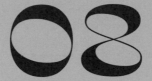

Great things happen as a result of a series of small things coming together.

Birthday Affirmation

Daily Affirmation

Sometimes, a change of self is needed more
than a change of scenery.

JANUARY

If trying harder isn't working for you,
try differently.

Birthday Affirmation

Daily Affirmation

You won't be broken by the load,
but by the way you choose to carry it.

JANUARY

Focus on the stars above rather
than the mud below.

Birthday Affirmation

Daily Affirmation

We can all shake the world even if we can
only do it in a gentle way.

JANUARY

The difference between ordinary and
extraordinary is that little 'extra'.

Birthday Affirmation

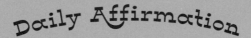

Daily Affirmation

Work hard, be kind and watch how amazing
things then happen for you.

JANUARY

12

Every day offers you the chance to choose
afresh how your story unfolds.

Birthday Affirmation

CAPRICORN

Daily Affirmation

Next time you feel you've been buried,
flip the idea and see what's been planted.

JANUARY

13

Keep your head up and
your heart hopeful.

Birthday Affirmation

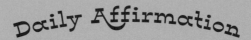

Daily Affirmation

Dark moments often
come with silver linings.

JANUARY

Wherever you go, take your
whole heart with you.

Birthday Affirmation

Daily Affirmation

The wise learn how they can turn their wounds into lasting wisdom.

JANUARY

15

Never be scared of your own power, own it and use it.

Birthday Affirmation

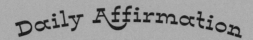
Daily Affirmation

You need to leave the place you were raised
in so you can see how big the world is.

JANUARY

16

There is nothing that can dim a light
that shines from within.

Birthday Affirmation

Daily Affirmation

Everyone who says 'No' to you will
help you find your true direction.

JANUARY

17

A winner is a dreamer who never
gave up on their dreams.

Birthday Affirmation

Don't be a prisoner to anything
you cannot change.

JANUARY

Listen to your heart, because it holds
the clue to your soul.

Birthday Affirmation

CAPRICORN

Daily Affirmation

Life can be very dull if you never take a risk.

JANUARY

Being clear about what you want makes
it easier for others to help you.

Birthday Affirmation

Daily Affirmation

Work hard on the art of listening
as it will reveal much.

JANUARY

20

You have feet in your shoes and can
steer yourself in any direction.

Birthday Affirmation

Daily Affirmation

Darkness cannot chase away darkness,
look to the light to do that.

JANUARY

21

Start your story today and enjoy
writing every word.

Birthday Affirmation

Today you have the chance to build
the tomorrow of your dreams.

JANUARY

22

Commit today to choosing to make the
best of the rest of your life.

Birthday Affirmation

AQUARIUS 37

Daily Affirmation

If you feel like giving up, just remember
all the people you need to prove wrong.

JANUARY

23

The wise know it's not about changing
the world, it's about changing yourself.

Birthday Affirmation

Daily Affirmation

Forget about chasing success and become,
instead, someone of real value.

JANUARY

24

There is nothing enlightened about being
a shrinking violet. You are meant to shine.

Birthday Affirmation

Daily Affirmation

The only person you ever need to try and be better than is who you were yesterday.

JANUARY

25

Be the one who encourages others and flourish in the energy of this.

Birthday Affirmation

The things that hurt you are also the things
that bless you because they change you.

JANUARY

26

Don't feel disappointed with what's not
achieved yet, but build on what you have.

Birthday Affirmation

AQUARIUS

Daily Affirmation

There are two important things you can
control, your work ethic and your attitude.

JANUARY

27

Welcome delays as a moment to pause,
rest and reset.

Birthday Affirmation

Daily Affirmation
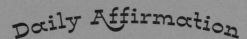

You may be disappointed if a plan fails
but more so if you didn't even try.

JANUARY

28

Aspire to your own dreams rather
than those of others.

Birthday Affirmation

AQUARIUS

Daily Affirmation

Action is the key to unlocking
what's possible.

JANUARY

29

Always question the status quo and form
your own opinions.

Birthday Affirmation

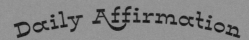

Daily Affirmation

A goal is really just a dream with
its deadline set by you.

JANUARY

30

If you want to become accomplished,
be motivated by something you truly love.

Birthday Affirmation

AQUARIUS

Daily Affirmation

Success is only valid if it accords
with your values and ideals.

JANUARY

31

Nothing grows without a seed and it takes
time and nurture to bloom.

Birthday Affirmation

Daily Affirmation

Ignore what could go wrong and focus
on what could go right.

FEBRUARY

Be remembered as the one who never
gave up on what mattered to them.

Birthday Affirmation

Daily Affirmation

Defeat is just a state of mind and you can
always change your mind.

FEBRUARY

02

Never regret anything, good days deliver
happiness and bad days experience.

Birthday Affirmation

Daily Affirmation

Walk alone and you may end up in amazing
places where nobody else has been.

FEBRUARY

03

Your struggles help identify
and develop your strengths.

Birthday Affirmation

AQUARIUS

Daily Affirmation

Flowers will grow back even after
the harshest of winters.

FEBRUARY

If you walk towards the sun you will
never be overshadowed.

Birthday Affirmation

The only difference between who you are and
who you want to be is what you do.

FEBRUARY

05

Have the patience to wait for what
you truly deserve, don't settle for less.

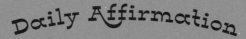

Birthday Affirmation

AQUARIUS

If you don't get in the game of life
and play, you won't win.

FEBRUARY

06

It is your decisions, not your circumstances,
that will reveal who you are.

Birthday Affirmation

Daily Affirmation

Pause when you feel tired,
take a rest to restore your resolve.

FEBRUARY

07

Every morning you wake up with the
opportunity to create the day you want.

Birthday Affirmation

Daily Affirmation

Character reveals itself by how we treat
people who can do nothing for us.

FEBRUARY

08

Create a meaningful life by simply looking
for the meaning that matters to you.

Birthday Affirmation

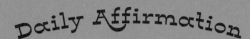

Daily Affirmation

Your world will end many times and then
start up again the following morning.

FEBRUARY

One day the story of what you went through
will inspire someone else's survival.

Birthday Affirmation

AQUARIUS

Daily Affirmation

If life gives you lemons, sweeten the juice
and share the optimism.

FEBRUARY

Be the hero of your own life.

Birthday Affirmation

Life isn't always easy but there's always scope
for worthwhile change.

FEBRUARY

Fear of the unknown is easily rectified.

Birthday Affirmation

Daily Affirmation

If someone is scared of your power,
that's about their weakness, not yours.

FEBRUARY

12

The door always opens to those
brave enough to knock.

Birthday Affirmation

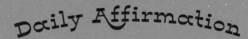

Daily Affirmation

Be loud and unapologetic about
what matters to you.

FEBRUARY

13

Whatever has happened, the story
must and will always go on.

Birthday Affirmation

Daily Affirmation

Expecting change with no effort from
you is like waiting for a ship at the airport.

FEBRUARY

Your future needs you. Your past does not.

Birthday Affirmation

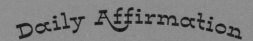

Daily Affirmation

Failure is just a big red flag telling you
to go in another direction.

FEBRUARY

15

Life is a series of thousands of tiny miracles and
your job is to notice them.

Birthday Affirmation

Daily Affirmation

Grow strong roots so that nothing can
destabilise you.

FEBRUARY

Work to create a better world for all
who live in it with you.

Birthday Affirmation

Daily Affirmation

When it feels like
nothing is going right, go left.

FEBRUARY

Invest in yourself to reap
the best dividends.

Birthday Affirmation

Daily Affirmation

Successful people succeed on purpose.

FEBRUARY

18

Know your own worth and be very clear
about how you expect to be treated.

Birthday Affirmation

Daily Affirmation

You are not lost, you are resetting your sails.

In your past, your younger self is so proud
of how far you have come.

Birthday Affirmation

Daily Affirmation

When you give the people you love
your attention, they blossom.

FEBRUARY

20

Pause, embrace the stillness and notice how
you don't have to be busy to feel alive.

Birthday Affirmation

♓

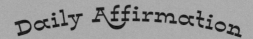

Daily Affirmation

You can distil all human wisdom to one
simple instruction: live in hope.

FEBRUARY

21

Stay open. Stay grounded.
Stay true to yourself.

Birthday Affirmation

Daily Affirmation

You won't find peace in your daily life
until you find it inside yourself.

FEBRUARY

22

Joy should be part of
the process, not the goal.

Birthday Affirmation

♓

Daily Affirmation

If your past is weighing you down,
imagine it lifting you up like a wave.

FEBRUARY

23

Give respect to the world and
everything in it, including yourself.

Birthday Affirmation

You cannot calm a storm, but you can wait calmly until it passes.

FEBRUARY

24

Expect the best from life and seek to ensure it through your daily commitment.

Birthday Affirmation

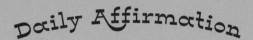

Daily Affirmation

Learn to say no – it's the biggest step you can take to keep control of your own life.

FEBRUARY

25

Don't put off until tomorrow what makes you happy today.

Birthday Affirmation

Daily Affirmation

The world is full of wonder, so look
to it to find meaning in your life.

FEBRUARY

26

Let go. And now let go some more.

Birthday Affirmation

Daily Affirmation

Set your priorities and allow others
to see what is important to you.

FEBRUARY

27

Invite serenity into your life and create
the space to let it grow.

Birthday Affirmation

PISCES

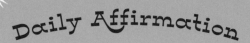

Daily Affirmation

You are in the driving seat
of your own destiny.

FEBRUARY

28

Hold up the candle or mirror to your life
– they both help spread the light.

Birthday Affirmation

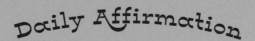

Daily Affirmation

Every day make a point of telling someone something you admire about them.

FEBRUARY

29

The wonder you felt as a child remains within and available to you.

Birthday Affirmation

Daily Affirmation

If you write down your plans and goals
you are more likely to achieve them.

MARCH

Pick a point a few years from now and imagine
how you want your life to be.

Birthday Affirmation

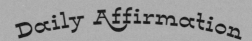

Daily Affirmation

The only way to have a more fulfilling life
is to work out what really matters to you.

MARCH

02

Think of the people who make you feel good
about yourself. Spend time with them.

Birthday Affirmation

Daily Affirmation

Learn to distinguish between the things you
can change and the things you can't.

MARCH

03

Simplify your life – it will give you the mental
clarity you need to reach your goals.

Birthday Affirmation

Life is not about avoiding hardships but learning to recognise and master them.

MARCH

Make a birthday list which reads, *'Today, I am thankful for ...'*

Birthday Affirmation

PISCES

Daily Affirmation

Happiness asks you only to let go of what you think life should be and accept what it is.

MARCH

05

You have as much light to shine in the world as anyone else.

Birthday Affirmation

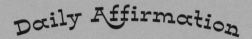

Daily Affirmation

Success is the place where preparation and
opportunity finally meet.

MARCH

Unlock the door to everything you have ever
wanted with a positive attitude.

Birthday Affirmation

Daily Affirmation

No matter how dark the nights,
the sun always rises.

MARCH

07

It is within your power to make the changes
you desire, so start small, grow big.

Birthday Affirmation

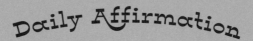

Daily Affirmation

Live less from habit and more from intent.

MARCH

08

Make yourself proud.

Birthday Affirmation

Shift the gears of your expectations by realising it's your experience that matters.

MARCH

Work towards the ultimate goal of spending life the way you want to spend it.

Birthday Affirmation

Wisdom is the reward
of hard-won experience.

MARCH

Become what you respect and mirror
what you admire.

Birthday Affirmation

Daily Affirmation

Life will always offer you another chance.
It is called tomorrow.

MARCH

Love and honour who you have become,
it has been hard won.

Birthday Affirmation

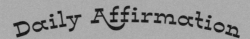

Daily Affirmation

The rarest flowers often bloom in the
harshest of environments.

MARCH

12

Never give up on yourself,
there's always another option.

Birthday Affirmation

Daily Affirmation

If you climb the mountain you'll be paving
the way for those behind you.

MARCH

13

Don't wait for the gift of flowers.
Plant your own.

Birthday Affirmation

♓

A happy life starts with a promise
to yourself to seek it.

MARCH

You are enough and have nothing
to prove to anyone.

Birthday Affirmation

Daily Affirmation

When you've gone as far as you think
you can go, take another step.

MARCH

15

Never underestimate yourself. It's only under
pressure that we show resilience.

Birthday Affirmation

Understand that with suffering come the life lessons that stand you in good stead.

MARCH

A hero is just an ordinary person who found the inner strength to continue.

PISCES

Daily Affirmation

If the world seems cold, chop wood
and light a fire.

MARCH

17

Courage is grace under pressure.

Birthday Affirmation

♓

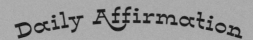

Daily Affirmation

Put your feet in the right place and
then be sure to stand firm.

MARCH

18

Find what makes you different because
that's also what makes you strong.

Birthday Affirmation

Daily Affirmation

Life doesn't get easier, but we can become
more resilient through experience.

MARCH

Let your hopes not your hurts shape
your future and guide you.

Birthday Affirmation

Daily Affirmation

Think kind thoughts. Say kind words.
Welcome kind deeds.

MARCH

20

Discover what sparks the light inside
you that will guide you on your way.

Birthday Affirmation

Daily Affirmation

Better to burn out and rest a while than have
no fire in your belly from the start.

MARCH

21

Walk with confidence even if that means
you have to fake it for a while.

Birthday Affirmation

Daily Affirmation

If it's not positive or kind, don't say it.

MARCH

22

Give thanks to all those who have helped
and supported you to get here.

Birthday Affirmation

Only make those promises you know
you can (and want to) keep.

MARCH

23

Stay true to yourself, forever and for all days.

♈

Daily Affirmation

Be open to alternative thoughts and ideas.

MARCH

24

Even the strongest reed will bend in the wind.

Birthday Affirmation

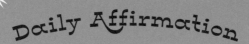

Daily Affirmation

Inspirational people share one common
characteristic – they all have courage.

MARCH

25

Stand tall. Reach high and
go up on tippy toes if that helps.

Birthday Affirmation

♈

Daily Affirmation

Challenge those around you to do their very
best, and show them how.

MARCH

26

Try to always excel at everything you do.

Birthday Affirmation

Daily Affirmation

Detachment doesn't mean you don't care,
it just means you stop trying to fix others.

MARCH

27

You are not stuck. You always have options,
which will allow you to grow.

Birthday Affirmation

Cultivate a deep empathy for all who cross
your path. You don't know their stories.

MARCH

28

Don't be afraid to use all of you to make
all the difference in the world.

Birthday Affirmation

Daily Affirmation

If you are feeling overwhelmed, break down
tasks into bite-sized chunks.

MARCH

Allow your generous nature to shine
forth and lead the way.

Birthday Affirmation

Daily Affirmation

Unleash your enthusiasm for your life,
your work, your loves, and inspire others.

MARCH

30

Dare to dream bigger and better
than yesterday.

Birthday Affirmation

Daily Affirmation

Allow yourself to invest in an optimistic
vision of your future.

MARCH

31

Take yourself and your needs seriously.

Birthday Affirmation

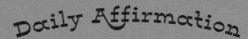

Daily Affirmation

Put aside the ego and focus instead on common goals for the greater good.

APRIL

Celebrate the success of others. If it can happen for them it can happen for you.

Birthday Affirmation

Daily Affirmation

Don't be afraid to show your vulnerabilities.
They are what make you human.

APRIL

02

Step out with high hopes and a happy heart.
All is as it should be.

Birthday Affirmation

♈

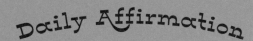

Daily Affirmation

Decide to make changes, where they are
needed, not excuses for inaction.

APRIL

03

Live by choice, not by random chance.

Birthday Affirmation

Daily Affirmation

A is for authenticity. Nobody likes a fraud.

APRIL

Be the person who has the courage to say what
everyone else in the room is thinking.

Birthday Affirmation

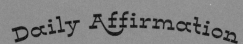

Daily Affirmation

Become the glue that holds others together
in community and goodness.

APRIL

05

Be happy with the person you woke
up as today, and radiate that positivity.

Birthday Affirmation

Daily Affirmation

If you want to find the flame to light your sacred fire, you will need to go on a quest.

APRIL

Honour all the people you are inspired by.

Birthday Affirmation

♈

The wings of transformation come from
patience and struggle. Ask a butterfly.

APRIL

Believing in yourself is a quality
that is attractive to others.

Birthday Affirmation

Daily Affirmation

Changing for the better is not some future
event, but a current activity.

APRIL

08

Personal growth is optional
but always rewarding.

Birthday Affirmation

114

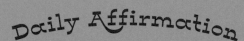

Daily Affirmation

If you want to succeed you'll need
to constantly adapt, revise and change.

APRIL

If you want to move forward, be honest with
yourself about what's holding you back.

Birthday Affirmation

Daily Affirmation

Times of great pain can also be times of great
transformation, even if you resist.

APRIL

10

Set the bar high and refuse to compromise
for anyone or anything.

Birthday Affirmation

Brick by brick, build the magic.

APRIL

11

You have every reason in the world to achieve the greatest of your dreams.

Birthday Affirmation

Daily Affirmation

They say time changes things, but remember
that it's not time that changes but you.

APRIL

12

Surprise drives progress, so make a promise
to surprise yourself more often.

Birthday Affirmation

Daily Affirmation

Failure is always a sign you are doing
something innovative.

APRIL

13

If you didn't have strong feelings – good and
bad ones – you'd be an automaton.

Birthday Affirmation

ARIES

Daily Affirmation

If you want to change something, create a new way that makes the old way obsolete.

APRIL

There is no joy in possession
if there is no sharing.

Birthday Affirmation

The fire of your purpose will have no problem
melting all obstacles on your path.

APRIL

Faith looks up and sees just
how far you can rise.

Birthday Affirmation

Friendships can leave a deeper mark on a life than love. Choose your friends wisely.

APRIL

Fall in love with yourself and open the door to that happiness.

Birthday Affirmation

Daily Affirmation

Respect anyone who tells you the truth,
however hard it is to hear.

APRIL

17

Keep your heart open and your
compassion close to hand.

Birthday Affirmation

Daily Affirmation

Be an open-minded and good-hearted
person and true friends will find you.

APRIL

Wisdom means knowing when it is time
to walk away and cut your losses.

Birthday Affirmation

Daily Affirmation

We can only feel sorrow for that which
has once given us great happiness.

APRIL

19

Keep on reinventing yourself.

Birthday Affirmation

Daily Affirmation

Get into the habit of ignoring gossip
and nonsense. You don't need either.

APRIL

20

When the winds of change blow,
build a windmill not a wall.

Birthday Affirmation

♈

A steadfast heart will
conquer all self-doubt.

APRIL

21

Keep your eyes on the sun and
you won't notice the shadows.

Birthday Affirmation

TAURUS

Daily Affirmation

Your obstacles may simply be the
darkness that precedes dawn.

APRIL

22

There's no need to add anything
to the mix in order for you to be happy.

Birthday Affirmation

♉

Daily Affirmation

Hardship often prepares ordinary people
for extraordinary lives.

APRIL

23

Find meaning in your life and you will
understand what it means to be happy.

Birthday Affirmation

Daily Affirmation

Nobody gets sent wisdom in a gift box,
you have to go out and discover it.

APRIL

24

Embrace yourself and your whole life
with both arms and a loving smile.

Birthday Affirmation

♈

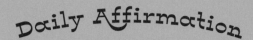

If it were not for hope,
the heart would break.

APRIL

25

Everything comes – in time –
to those who know how to wait.

Birthday Affirmation

TAURUS

Hard work trumps talent – every time.

APRIL

26

Never be too proud to weep, too serious
to laugh or too selfish to help out.

Birthday Affirmation

Good judgement comes from experience,
which usually comes from bad judgement.

APRIL

27

Make honesty the first chapter
in the book of your life.

Birthday Affirmation

Daily Affirmation

Watch, pay attention, persevere and
work hard and you will succeed.

APRIL

28

Every life will have its sorrows and often
these will be what awaken us.

Birthday Affirmation

Daily Affirmation

You can always choose 'Hope'
as an act of wilfulness.

APRIL

29

Every journey you will ever take starts
with one small step.

Birthday Affirmation

Daily Affirmation

Always believe tomorrow will be better;
it will help you bear any hardship today.

APRIL

30

When the student is ready,
the teacher will find them.

Birthday Affirmation

Daily Affirmation

Aim for excellence, not perfection.

MAY

01

Find things to be thankful for
and be humbled by how long that list is.

Birthday Affirmation

Daily Affirmation

You have become wise when you know the
proper use for your time and talent.

MAY

02

Knowing your authentic self
is true enlightenment.

Birthday Affirmation

What we resist persists until we face it.

MAY

03

The longer you focus, the clearer the path.

Birthday Affirmation

TAURUS

Daily Affirmation

The way to take sorrow out of death
is to grab love out of life.

MAY

04

You already know what to do next.
You just have to listen.

Birthday Affirmation

♈

Daily Affirmation

Have the courage to make mistakes
because it allows you to grow.

MAY

05

Give yourself permission to seek
out your own reality.

Birthday Affirmation

Daily Affirmation

Adversity can be a wake-up call to do what your heart has wanted all along.

MAY

06

Follow your instincts and inner intelligence.

Birthday Affirmation

♈

Daily Affirmation

One day you will see that nothing was in vain.

MAY

07

Let go of everything you are not
and cherish what you are.

Birthday Affirmation

Daily Affirmation

Pain is often the door through which we walk
to find what we need on the other side.

MAY

08

You will be forever known by the footsteps
you take and the tracks you leave.

Birthday Affirmation

Daily Affirmation

Work out what's not true so that you
can be sure of what is.

MAY

Flow with ease by following
your own nature.

Birthday Affirmation

Daily Affirmation

Educating the mind but forgetting to educate
the heart is no education at all.

MAY

10

All peace lies within you, so pause to find it.

Birthday Affirmation

♉

Optimism is the cornerstone
of real achievement.

MAY

Fan the inner sparks of possibility
into flames of success.

Birthday Affirmation

TAURUS

Daily Affirmation

You may need to become lost in order
to really find yourself again.

MAY

12

What you think is what you will become.

Birthday Affirmation

♉

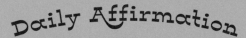
Daily Affirmation

The only thing you have ultimate power
and control over is your own thoughts.

MAY

13

No freedom is ever given, it is always
worked for and won.

Birthday Affirmation

Daily Affirmation

Every single accomplishment starts
with a decision to try.

MAY

You are capable of more than
you can ever imagine.

Birthday Affirmation

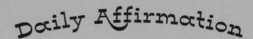

Daily Affirmation

Everything worth having demands pain,
effort and difficulty.

MAY

15

Keep your eyes open – nobody can
hit the target with them closed.

Birthday Affirmation

TAURUS

151

Don't be sad that something is over,
be happy that it happened.

MAY

Don't ask for easy, ask for amazing.

Don't get to the end of the road without having won some victory for living things.

MAY

17

Cheerfulness is a sign of hard-won wisdom and gratitude.

Birthday Affirmation

Daily Affirmation

The heavier your heart,
the stronger you will climb.

MAY

18

Find a purpose to serve rather
than a lifestyle to live.

Birthday Affirmation

Daily Affirmation

Life's biggest prize is the chance to work hard at something you love doing.

MAY

19

Hope is the fruit that comes from taking ownership of your life.

Birthday Affirmation

Daily Affirmation

Happiness depends on being free,
and being free requires courage.

MAY

20

In all things, demand the
very best of yourself.

Birthday Affirmation

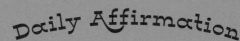

Daily Affirmation

The lightest heart will carry
the heaviest weight.

MAY

21

Be happy in this moment,
and kind whenever possible.

Birthday Affirmation

Daily Affirmation

Keep a buoyant and cheerful frame
of mind and success will follow.

MAY

22

The energy you extend is equal to that which
returns, so make it positive.

Birthday Affirmation

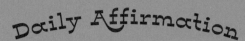

Daily Affirmation

Spend longer seeing the good side
of life than you do seeing the bad.

MAY

23

Actively seek the fun in life today and relish it.

Birthday Affirmation

Most of the problems that worry
you will never actually materialise.

MAY

24

Nobody ever hurt their eyes
by looking on the bright side.

Birthday Affirmation

Daily Affirmation

Nobody needs a key to happiness
because its door is always open.

MAY

25

Look for joy in your own heart,
and not in your circumstances.

Birthday Affirmation

Daily Affirmation

Never let the fear of losing keep
you from being in the game.

MAY

26

Make living your best life
a focus every day.

Birthday Affirmation

♊

Daily Affirmation

It's not how long you will live
but how well that really matters.

MAY

27

Make a plan to set off today
and find your destiny.

Birthday Affirmation

Daily Affirmation

Everything negative that comes your way
comes with the chance to rise above it.

MAY

28

You'll only understand life's important
lessons by living through them.

Birthday Affirmation

Daily Affirmation

The best thing about your life will
be all your quiet acts of kindness.

MAY

29

Look hard enough and you will always find
something to smile about.

Birthday Affirmation

Daily Affirmation

Life expands in direct proportion
to your courage in living it.

MAY

30

Your life will be what you decide to make it.

Birthday Affirmation

♊

Daily Affirmation

Live your dreams, not your fears.

MAY

31

Don't waste one more heartbeat
on things that don't matter.

Birthday Affirmation

Don't waste a life waiting for the
storm that may never come.

JUNE

Stay around long enough and life
will show you how to live it well.

Birthday Affirmation

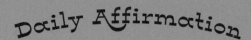
Daily Affirmation

You will go precisely as far as your
mind lets you.

JUNE

02

Thank other people for their limitations
and hand them back. They're not yours.

Birthday Affirmation

Daily Affirmation

The choices you make
tell people who you are.

JUNE

03

You have two hands, one to help yourself
and one to help others.

Birthday Affirmation

Daily Affirmation

If you want to see yourself clearly,
see how others react to you.

JUNE

Never lose faith in humanity –
yours or other people's.

Birthday Affirmation

Daily Affirmation

If you just sit back and allow life to happen,
it's hard to accomplish your goals.

JUNE

05

All the great blessings are within
you and within your reach.

Birthday Affirmation

Daily Affirmation

Allow your greatest pains to transform
into your greatest strengths.

JUNE

Be happy in this moment;
this moment is your life.

Birthday Affirmation

Make your day, make your life.

JUNE

07

Your best weapon in life is a kind
and gentle spirit.

Birthday Affirmation

Daily Affirmation

Your past will never define you, but it will
prepare you for what lies ahead.

JUNE

08

There's nothing more attractive
than a grateful and loving heart.

Birthday Affirmation

 Daily Affirmation

Once a day, disconnect from all the noise
and distractions and sit with you.

JUNE

 09

The more you celebrate your life, the
more you'll find worth celebrating.

Birthday Affirmation

Ⅱ

Think of life as like an echo sending
back what you've given out.

JUNE

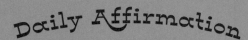

10

Find all the people who make you
a better person and hang on to them.

Birthday Affirmation

Daily Affirmation

Let the breath you take inspire you and then
breathe out with love.

JUNE

Each new day is an opportunity to start
again with joy.

Birthday Affirmation

♊

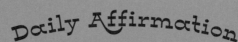
You are not your thoughts, so allow them
to come and go without fear.

JUNE

12

Press pause for a moment and relish
your place in the world.

Birthday Affirmation

Daily Affirmation

Every moment offers a new beginning.
Every moment. No exceptions.

JUNE

13

You will always have a say in how you
respond to what happens to you.

Birthday Affirmation

Go boldly through your past to get
to the next level of your present.

JUNE

Some will build you up, others tear you down.
One day you'll thank both.

Birthday Affirmation

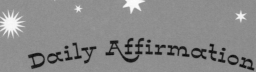

Daily Affirmation

If you don't change you don't grow, and if you
don't grow you are not living.

JUNE

15

You're not being asked to be the best,
just to try your best.

Birthday Affirmation

Ⅱ

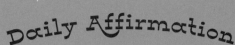

Daily Affirmation

Every life will be a pile of good things and a pile of bad. They don't cancel each other out.

JUNE

Enjoy everything that's happening because it means you're truly alive.

Birthday Affirmation

Tell your heart each new day
is the very best day.

JUNE

17

By simply being alive, you are
a real-life miracle.

Birthday Affirmation

Daily Affirmation

You won't learn from anything that comes
out of your mouth, so learn to listen.

JUNE

18

Every day is a cheerful invitation
to get up and get going.

Birthday Affirmation

Something special waits for you in every day.
Your job is to find it.

JUNE

You can and you will find the help you need
along the way.

Birthday Affirmation

Daily Affirmation

Start over today and make a new ending,
one you can be proud of.

JUNE

20

It doesn't matter what pace you go at,
as long as you keep going.

Birthday Affirmation

Daily Affirmation

Remember the good moments of your
childhood and look towards their fulfilment.

JUNE

21

Reflect on the intentions you want to set
for your personal new year.

Birthday Affirmation

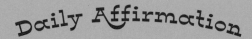

Daily Affirmation

Seek counsel from those who speak
to your nurturing self.

JUNE

22

Every day is a new opportunity to renew
your personal energy.

Birthday Affirmation

CANCER

A compassionate heart starts with one's self.

JUNE

23

Your ability to get things done is a daily
renewal of graft and application.

Birthday Affirmation

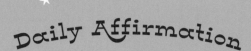
Daily Affirmation

Your feelings are your own, to reflect on as they pass through your internal landscape.

JUNE

24

Celebrate your efforts as well as your achievements.

Birthday Affirmation

CANCER

Daily Affirmation

Be empathetic to others but not
overwhelmed by their needs.

JUNE

25

Honour your enthusiasm for those
aspects of life that enrich you.

Birthday Affirmation

Daily Affirmation

Worrying about what you can't change
is wasted energy: focus on what you can.

JUNE

26

Success begins with inspiration
and continues with effort.

Birthday Affirmation

Daily Affirmation

Don't run from occasional solitude,
it will yield its own reward.

JUNE

27

Seek contentment as much
as happiness in your daily life.

Birthday Affirmation

♋

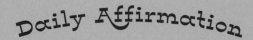

Daily Affirmation

Make positivity your default, it will determine
how well you achieve your aim.

JUNE

28

Take pleasure in simple joys today and all days.

Birthday Affirmation

CANCER

195

Find your happiness by asking someone else
what they need and helping them.

JUNE

29

Turn your 'I can't' to 'I can' and start
making those long-term plans.

Birthday Affirmation

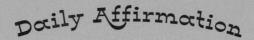

Daily Affirmation

Looking outside yourself is dreaming,
looking inside is awakening.

JUNE

30

Look inside yourself to find all the beauty
and love you've been seeking.

Birthday Affirmation

Daily Affirmation

When you are truly present, you become real,
life becomes real, others become real.

JULY

01

Give yourself the gift of not fearing life
and liberate the possibilities.

Birthday Affirmation

Daily Affirmation

Don't spend so long looking at a closed door
that you miss another one opening.

JULY

02

Think about what your skills are,
and how you can now best use them.

Birthday Affirmation

CANCER

Daily Affirmation

Decide to just stop criticising anyone,
including and especially yourself.

JULY

03

Give yourself permission to 'just be', which
is the best way to become all you can be.

Birthday Affirmation

Daily Affirmation

Remember that the very act of loving takes
you on to the path of apprenticeship.

JULY

04

Love where and when you can and expect
its return in kind if not in full.

Birthday Affirmation

Daily Affirmation

Allowing yourself to feel things deeply is an
invitation to your future to come closer.

JULY

05

To be courageous in life is to stay faithful
to the unique way you were made.

Birthday Affirmation

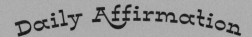
Daily Affirmation

You are always en route to becoming
your best self, but you have to keep the faith
when the track is dark.

JULY

06

Each birthday you stand at the frontier
between who you were and who you'll be.

Birthday Affirmation

Daily Affirmation

A fixed idea of happiness can block
what will really make you happy.

JULY

07

Look for all the opportunities for joy
that are right under your nose today.

Birthday Affirmation

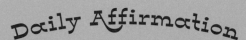

Daily Affirmation

A pot in search of a lid will always feel empty
and forget that it can still boil water.

JULY

08

The world will touch you in many ways, ensuring
your presence matters.

Birthday Affirmation

CANCER

Daily Affirmation

True happiness always demands
determination, effort and time.

JULY

Lasting change doesn't happen overnight,
so work patiently towards all your goals.

Birthday Affirmation

The only true constant in life is change.
All things change, nothing stays the same.

JULY

10

Identify the positive changes you want
in your life and take a step towards them.

Birthday Affirmation

CANCER

Daily Affirmation

Negative thoughts and feelings are not an
intrinsic part of your mind, they'll pass.

JULY

Make a promise to find time for silence and
create the place where you will meet yourself.

Birthday Affirmation

Give the gift of your full attention to whatever
you're doing and whoever you're with.

JULY

12

Today is a new day and tomorrow will be too.
This is the gift that keeps giving.

Birthday Affirmation

A bird is born with the ability to fly
but it still needs to learn how.

JULY

13

Spread your wings, trust your talents
and see where they can take you.

Birthday Affirmation

Stepping out of your comfort zone can be scary
but will make you feel alive again.

JULY

14

The only thing you will ever truly own is your
own story, and your only job is to live it.

Birthday Affirmation

CANCER

Daily Affirmation

Life offers you choices all the time; it's up to
you which of them you accept or decline.

JULY

15

Invest in you. If you need to learn something
to realise a dream, go back to school.

Birthday Affirmation

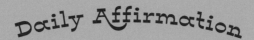
Daily Affirmation

There's no rule book, except the one in your head, saying you have to settle for less.

JULY

16

Don't waste another day thinking
'I wish I'd done that.' Do it today.

Birthday Affirmation

CANCER

Daily Affirmation

Mistakes offer us something very precious –
a learning curve.

JULY

17

Life is what happens when you are busy
looking the other way.

Birthday Affirmation

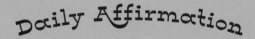

Daily Affirmation

Optimism and hard work make the world go round, and anyone can have them.

JULY

18

Run the race of life looking forwards, never backwards.

Birthday Affirmation

CANCER

Steer clear of anyone who is not
comfortable with you being you.

JULY

Find three different ways you can say 'yes'
to life as you celebrate your birthday.

Birthday Affirmation

Daily Affirmation

You're not supposed to know what happens next. Where would the fun be in that?

JULY

20

Don't just give your power away to others, you will need it to achieve great things.

Birthday Affirmation

CANCER

A pile of rocks is nothing more until someone
imagines building a great cathedral.

JULY

21

Believe you are someone special so that you
can then be that someone special.

Birthday Affirmation

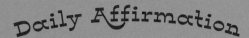

Daily Affirmation

There's no such thing as failure. Either you'll win or you'll learn a valuable lesson.

JULY

22

Be so damn good they can't ignore you.

Birthday Affirmation

Daily Affirmation

Don't waste time watching the clock, but do
what it does and keep going. Always.

JULY

23

If you can dream it then you can
do it, so make sure you dream big.

Birthday Affirmation

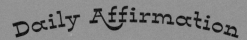

Daily Affirmation

Strive always for progress,
not impossible perfection.

JULY

24

With a new birthday comes new ideas and new
strengths to push and guide you on.

Birthday Affirmation

If it feels like the end, you can be sure you are
at the beginning.

JULY

25

Those things that you feel excited about
give you a big clue about your purpose.

Birthday Affirmation

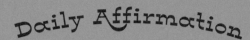

Daily Affirmation

Start now. Use what you have
and do what you can.

JULY

26

Get busy living the biggest, the best
and the fullest life that you can.

Birthday Affirmation

Daily Affirmation

Many things will seem impossible but
only until you have done them.

JULY

27

Wake up feeling determined and
go to bed feeling satisfied.

Birthday Affirmation

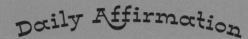

Daily Affirmation

It's always a good day
to have the best ever day.

JULY

28

You don't have to allow anyone else
to decide who you are, that's your job.

Birthday Affirmation

Daily Affirmation

Life is 10 per cent about what happens to you,
the rest is how you react.

JULY

29

If you've not yet found your passion,
keep looking until you find it.

Birthday Affirmation

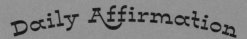

Daily Affirmation

Tomorrow's not here, yesterday's gone but
right now is always a good time to start.

JULY
30

Ask yourself if what you're doing now is getting
you closer to what you want to do.

Birthday Affirmation

Daily Affirmation

Don't compare your life to others'. You may still be on chapter 5, while they're on chapter 20.

JULY

31

No butterfly got beautiful by hiding in its cocoon. Now is your time to shine.

Birthday Affirmation

Daily Affirmation

Every successful person starts out with the belief they can make the world better.

AUGUST

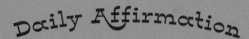

01

It may feel like a small step, but one day you'll look back and see it was a huge leap.

Birthday Affirmation

Daily Affirmation

A smooth sea never made
a skilful sailor.

AUGUST

02

If you want to partner with hope
and opportunity, get yourself out
on the dance floor.

Birthday Affirmation

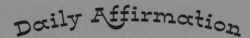

Daily Affirmation

If you want to be happy, remember
to be alert to all the blessings of life.

AUGUST

03

The way you live your life is your message to
the world, so make it an inspiring one.

Birthday Affirmation

Daily Affirmation

Don't put your problems in charge of your life,
let your dreams lead the way.

AUGUST

Keep putting your best foot forward
and see how the best is yet to come.

Birthday Affirmation

Daily Affirmation

Some people want it to happen, some people
wish it and some just make it happen.

AUGUST

If life is a big canvas then your job is to paint it,
using all the colours available to you.

Birthday Affirmation

LEO

Daily Affirmation

Have you ever noticed how the wrong choices can bring us to the right places?

AUGUST

It takes courage to grow into who you really are, so remember to reward your efforts.

Birthday Affirmation

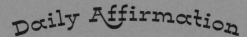

Daily Affirmation

Never be afraid to fail, be afraid
of never having tried.

AUGUST

07

Do more of what makes you happy –
a lot more.

Birthday Affirmation

LEO

Daily Affirmation

Mix effort and courage with purpose and
direction and you'll have the life you want.

AUGUST

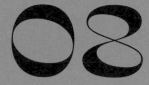

Know you can create the real 'self' you'll be
happy to spend the rest of your life with.

Birthday Affirmation

Daily Affirmation

Find the courage to always follow your
own heart and intuitive hunches.

AUGUST

Everything you need will find you just
as long as you promise to keep going.

Birthday Affirmation

LEO

237

Daily Affirmation

If it doesn't enhance your life
it doesn't belong in your life.

AUGUST

10

Have a good day, but trust and believe that
your best day ever hasn't happened yet.

Birthday Affirmation

Daily Affirmation

It takes a dark night to really show
off the brightest stars.

AUGUST

Always try to take the scenic route
and really notice what's around you.

Birthday Affirmation

Daily Affirmation

Speed is irrelevant. Ask a tortoise or a snail.
All that counts is moving forward.

AUGUST

12

You won't find your own greatness in what
you have, because it lies in what you give.

Birthday Affirmation

Daily Affirmation

Nobody grows when things are easy.
We all grow through the tough times.

AUGUST

13

Know your true worth and remember
to increase its interest daily.

Birthday Affirmation

LEO

If you see something beautiful in another person, let them know.

AUGUST

Keep hold of what feels important and let the rest fall into place or away from you.

Birthday Affirmation

Daily Affirmation

When life lands you in a tough spot, don't say
'why me?', say 'ok, try me.'

AUGUST

Get out of your head and out of your way
and let yourself celebrate being YOU today.

Birthday Affirmation

Daily Affirmation

Try to stop feeling afraid of what might go wrong and think about what might go right.

AUGUST

Be an agent of grace and goodness and see what a difference it makes.

Birthday Affirmation

Daily Affirmation

If you practise you'll learn to dance over and
away from crushing disappointments.

AUGUST

The old ways won't open any new doors,
so look for new ways of doing things.

Birthday Affirmation

Daily Affirmation

Do something today that the future
you will thank you for.

AUGUST

Thoughts are just seeds, so what do you
want to grow? Flowers or weeds?

Birthday Affirmation

Daily Affirmation

Watch the magic that occurs when you allow
you, and others, to be who you truly are.

AUGUST

You will grow immeasurably through all the
people you meet and the places you go.

Birthday Affirmation

LEO

Daily Affirmation

Trusting in yourself may be the hardest lesson
but it is also the most rewarding.

AUGUST

20

Life is not what you're given but what you
create, conquer and achieve.

Birthday Affirmation

248

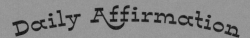

Daily Affirmation

Try going the extra mile –
there's always room for one more.

AUGUST

21

Gratitude will always turn what you already
have into more than enough.

Birthday Affirmation

LEO

Success is a journey, not a destination.

AUGUST

22

If you want to fly, shake off everything
that weighs you down.

Birthday Affirmation

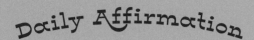
Daily Affirmation

Be willing to start each new day
as a complete beginner.

AUGUST

23

It is never too late to become who
you could have been.

Birthday Affirmation

VIRGO

Daily Affirmation

Change your decisions, change your life.

AUGUST

24

Set your goals – there's no telling what will happen when you act on them.

Birthday Affirmation

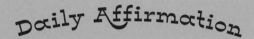

Daily Affirmation

In the darkest hour you'll be able to see the
brilliance of the light within.

AUGUST

25

You can decide for yourself what and who you
want to be, and then just go and be it.

Birthday Affirmation

Daily Affirmation

Whatever it is you are seeking will not come
in the way you are expecting.

AUGUST

26

Stay open to all opportunities lining up for you
now, especially the unexpected ones.

Birthday Affirmation

♍

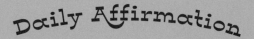
Daily Affirmation

A comeback is a hundred times more
powerful than any setback.

AUGUST

27

Love your life and it will love you right back.

Birthday Affirmation

Daily Affirmation

Your mind is the only thing that can limit
you if you allow it to.

AUGUST

28

The grass is always greener where
you decide to water it.

Birthday Affirmation

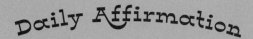
Daily Affirmation

Decide to do more things every day that make
you forget to check your phone.

AUGUST

29

Remember to tell yourself regularly,
'I can, and I will.'

Birthday Affirmation

Daily Affirmation

Empower yourself by walking quietly away from anything that no longer serves you.

AUGUST

30

Once things change inside you, they soon start to change around you.

Birthday Affirmation

Daily Affirmation

The thing you are most afraid of doing
may be the very thing that sets you free.

AUGUST

31

Be enough for yourself –
everyone else can wait.

Birthday Affirmation

Everything will come to you at exactly the right time, so practise patience.

SEPTEMBER

Forget the plan. Breathe. Trust.
And then see what happens.

Birthday Affirmation

♍

Daily Affirmation

Some get burned by the fire, but some
will rise from the ashes like a phoenix.

SEPTEMBER

02

Spend time with the people who push
you hard to be your very best self.

Birthday Affirmation

Daily Affirmation

Find the courage to let go of what you cannot change, and happiness will follow.

SEPTEMBER

03

Remember who you are and as soon as you do, watch the game change.

Birthday Affirmation

Today is that tomorrow you were
talking about yesterday.

SEPTEMBER

Stay open to what is different
and surprising, and embrace it.

Birthday Affirmation

Daily Affirmation

You may fall and break,
but you then rise and heal.

SEPTEMBER

05

It should be easy to trust the next chapter
of your life, because you are its author.

Birthday Affirmation

Daily Affirmation

Everything you are going through now
is preparing you for what you want.

SEPTEMBER

Decide today how you want your life
to be, and never look back.

Birthday Affirmation

Daily Affirmation

Nothing is forever, which means you can rise
from anything and recreate yourself.

SEPTEMBER

07

Everything is now up to you – every thought,
every feeling, every moment.

Birthday Affirmation

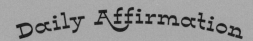

Daily Affirmation

Be happy with what you already have
and work hard for what you want.

SEPTEMBER

Invest in yourself. Love unconditionally
and dream as big as you can.

Birthday Affirmation

Daily Affirmation

You'll find yourself in the things that truly
inspire you, so never stop looking for them.

SEPTEMBER

Flowers need time to blossom
and so do you.

Birthday Affirmation

♍

Not all changes feel positive at first,
you may need to trust the process.

SEPTEMBER

10

You were not created to be defeated
but to be victorious in your life.

Daily Affirmation

A bird in a tree does not have to fear the branch may break because she has wings.

SEPTEMBER

Make like a wildflower and grow in all the places people never thought you'd thrive.

Birthday Affirmation

Daily Affirmation

You don't need to see the whole staircase
to climb the first stair.

SEPTEMBER

12

One day you will be able to look back
and see how all the time you were blooming.

Birthday Affirmation

Daily Affirmation

Nothing is as strong as gentleness and nothing
as gentle as true strength.

SEPTEMBER

13

Expect nothing and appreciate everything.

Birthday Affirmation

You can scream and cry but let this outrage
fuel your progress, not halt it.

SEPTEMBER

14

Accept what is, let go of what was and trust
with your whole heart in what will come.

Birthday Affirmation

You change the world by example,
not by sharing your opinions.

SEPTEMBER

You are always just one choice away
from a brand-new vision of life.

Birthday Affirmation

Daily Affirmation

It is OK to outgrow those people who
are no longer growing as you are.

SEPTEMBER

Be messy and complicated and even uncertain,
but make sure you show up anyway.

Birthday Affirmation

If you want to thrive, create new habits
and leave survival mode behind.

SEPTEMBER

Trust in the magic of brand-new beginnings.

Birthday Affirmation

Daily Affirmation

Be patient when you have nothing
and grateful when you have everything.

SEPTEMBER

18

Life wants to make you happy but will
first want to make you strong.

Birthday Affirmation

VIRGO

 Daily Affirmation

We attract what we are, not what we want,
so if you want great be great.

SEPTEMBER

Your strength has come from overcoming
the things you thought would finish you.

Birthday Affirmation

♍

Our words can be powerful,
but it is our actions that shape lives.

SEPTEMBER

20

If you want change, focus all your
energy on building the new.

Birthday Affirmation

The quieter we are
the more we can hear.

SEPTEMBER

21

Be more snail and slow down
to really enjoy your life.

Birthday Affirmation

Daily Affirmation

You are not responsible for the happiness of others, only your own.

SEPTEMBER

22

Find the courage to live your life the way you want to, not as others might wish.

Birthday Affirmation

Daily Affirmation

The only person who can give your
life meaning is you.

SEPTEMBER

23

You can't cross the ocean without losing
sight of the shore. Take a leap.

Birthday Affirmation

One day, as you look back with hard-won wisdom, everything will make perfect sense.

SEPTEMBER

24

Life may turn out differently from what you expected, but learn to adapt and all will be well.

Birthday Affirmation

Daily Affirmation

Everything ends – youth, life, love –
and that's why they are so valuable.

SEPTEMBER

25

Cherish the people who see your quirks
and say 'me too!' This is your tribe.

Birthday Affirmation

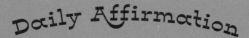
Daily Affirmation

Sometimes only a big shake-up will land
us in the place we are meant to be.

SEPTEMBER

26

Don't look back – you are not going that way.

Birthday Affirmation

Daily Affirmation

You will learn that the most impressive
personalities carry the most painful scars.

SEPTEMBER

27

New energy is entering your life,
and this will fuel your progress.

Birthday Affirmation

♎

Daily Affirmation

What if you've been given this mountain to climb to show others it can be done?

SEPTEMBER

28

You may find what you are looking for or you may find something much better.

Birthday Affirmation

People don't cross your path by accident,
you are meant to meet everyone you meet.

SEPTEMBER

Don't let anyone steal
your joy away from you.

Behind every face is a human who could
probably do with a little more kindness.

SEPTEMBER

30

Today you can start the future
you created yesterday.

Birthday Affirmation

Daily Affirmation

Some storms come not to disrupt your
life but to clear your path.

OCTOBER

If it doesn't open it's not the door
for you: look for another one.

Birthday Affirmation

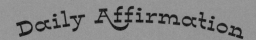
Daily Affirmation

If it feels like an uphill struggle, keep going
by imagining the view from the top.

OCTOBER

02

Make today the kind of day when you can
see the light shining out of everything.

Birthday Affirmation

Daily Affirmation

People can inspire or drain you – choose wisely.

OCTOBER

03

Let go of the past and allow it to let go of you.

Birthday Affirmation

Daily Affirmation

When you feel like quitting,
remember why you started.

OCTOBER

04

You did not get out of bed
today to be mediocre.

Birthday Affirmation

Daily Affirmation

Don't react, take a deep breath
and then respond.

OCTOBER

05

Once you see your own true worth, you won't
want to be around those who don't.

Birthday Affirmation

♎

You won't find passion if you insist on playing small and settling for less.

OCTOBER

Some memories never leave but become an important part of you.

Birthday Affirmation

You are writing your legacy every day,
so make it count.

OCTOBER

07

Surround yourself with the dreamers and the
doers, the thinkers and the believers.

Birthday Affirmation

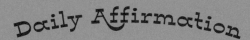
Daily Affirmation

It may feel as if nothing is certain, but that just means everything is possible.

OCTOBER

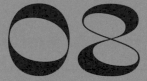

Let go of what's behind you so that you can reach forward for what's in front.

Birthday Affirmation

Daily Affirmation

If you don't step forward you will always
be stuck in the same place.

OCTOBER

Make a promise to create beauty in your life,
no matter what it takes.

Birthday Affirmation

Daily Affirmation

If you have known despair, you
have learned to value hope.

OCTOBER

10

Blessings are coming.
Just ask for them.

Birthday Affirmation

LIBRA

299

Daily Affirmation

How you walk with the broken says everything
that is important about you.

OCTOBER

Try to enjoy where you are now because you'll
be moving on before long.

Birthday Affirmation

Daily Affirmation

The world is full of beautiful places.
Make sure your heart is one of them.

OCTOBER

12

Remember to give thanks to everyone
who's made a difference in your life.

Birthday Affirmation

LIBRA

Daily Affirmation

Travel far enough to meet yourself.

OCTOBER

13

Don't worry about what can happen in a year,
just focus on the next 24 hours.

Birthday Affirmation

Daily Affirmation

It might take you 10 years to get to
the one year that will change your life.

OCTOBER

Do it for you.

Birthday Affirmation

Daily Affirmation

Recovery is a slow process that takes time, patience and hope.

OCTOBER

If something aligns with your purpose, go for it.

Birthday Affirmation

Daily Affirmation

Your current situation is never
your final destination.

OCTOBER

You might need to get a little
bit lost to find a better path.

Birthday Affirmation

Integrity is everything.
Everything!

OCTOBER

If it is right for you it will happen.
When it does, give thanks.

Birthday Affirmation

Daily Affirmation

The days that threaten to break you are the days that end up making you.

OCTOBER

18

Sometimes, not getting what you want turns out to be a wonderful stroke of luck.

Birthday Affirmation

Whatever comes, let it come, whatever goes,
let it go, whatever stays, let it stay.

OCTOBER

A great attitude will ensure a great day,
then a great month and then a great year.

Birthday Affirmation

Daily Affirmation

Never become chained to a mind-numbing
routine that kills your dreams.

OCTOBER

20

The greatest risk you can ever take is to allow
people to see who you really are.

Birthday Affirmation

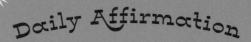

Daily Affirmation

If people throw stones your way, gather them
up and build an empire.

OCTOBER

21

You have a quiet voice inside that doesn't
use words. Learn how to listen to it.

Birthday Affirmation

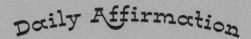

Daily Affirmation

Where you come from does not matter,
it's where you're going that counts.

OCTOBER

22

Think about all that you are instead
of all that you're not.

Birthday Affirmation

Daily Affirmation

Life is like a camera lens, you just need
to focus on what is important.

OCTOBER

23

Happiness will come from your
own decisions and actions.

Birthday Affirmation

♏

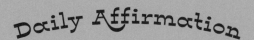

Daily Affirmation

The best things in the world cannot be seen –
they have to be felt in the heart.

OCTOBER

24

Believe you can and you will be halfway there.

Birthday Affirmation

SCORPIO

313

Daily Affirmation

Judge each day not by the harvest you reap
but by the seeds you sow.

OCTOBER

25

Today, choose life with all its challenges,
joys, happiness and pain.

Birthday Affirmation

♏

Daily Affirmation

The secret of success is to put all of you,
mind, body and soul, into every act.

OCTOBER

26

Let go of the life you planned so you can
accept and welcome the one waiting for you.

Birthday Affirmation

Daily Affirmation

Always allow your reach to exceed
and extend beyond your grasp.

OCTOBER

27

Your circumstances don't dictate how far you
can go, they're just a starting point.

Birthday Affirmation

♏

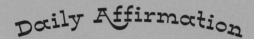

Daily Affirmation

Everything behind and in front of you is nothing
compared with what lies inside you.

OCTOBER

28

Learn to be still so that life
can happen within that stillness.

Birthday Affirmation

Daily Affirmation

Your decisions
shape your destiny.

OCTOBER

29

Your life is your very own adventure, so stay
positive whatever comes your way.

Birthday Affirmation

♏

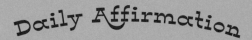

Daily Affirmation

Don't dwell in the past or hanker for the future,
but concentrate on the 'now'.

OCTOBER

30

Don't just 'go' through life, but always
try and 'grow' through life.

Birthday Affirmation

Play all the cards you are holding.

OCTOBER

31

Life is not about finding yourself,
it is about creating yourself.

Birthday Affirmation

♏

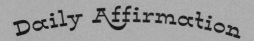

Daily Affirmation

Success is learning to want only what you need.

NOVEMBER

Our time on earth is precious, so don't rush
but make time to smell the flowers.

Birthday Affirmation

Daily Affirmation

You don't plan a life, you make yourself
available for its opportunities.

NOVEMBER

Do as much good as you can, and you will find
happiness gravitates towards you.

Birthday Affirmation

♏

Daily Affirmation

Always keep your eyes open, because you
never know what may inspire you.

NOVEMBER

03

If the plan is not working, change
it, but always stick to the goal.

Birthday Affirmation

SCORPIO

Nothing will ever grow in your comfort
zone, so be brave and step out of it.

NOVEMBER

Take all your dreams seriously,
they are your best hope for the future.

Birthday Affirmation

♏

Happiness is not something
'out there', it is within you.

NOVEMBER

05

You can't change the direction of the wind,
but you can adjust your sails.

SCORPIO

Daily Affirmation

Choosing change may not be comfortable
or easy, but it is always worth the risk.

NOVEMBER

You are never too old
to dream a new dream.

Birthday Affirmation

♏

Today's achievements
were yesterday's dreams.

NOVEMBER

Keep facing the sun and the shadows
will stay behind you.

Birthday Affirmation

SCORPIO

Daily Affirmation

Don't allow yesterday to swallow
up too much of today.

NOVEMBER

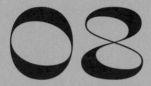

08

Trust that while you may go where you
intended, you'll end up where you need to be.

Birthday Affirmation

♏

Daily Affirmation

Stop talking about what you want
to do and start doing it.

NOVEMBER

An optimist sees the opportunity
in everything.

Birthday Affirmation

Daily Affirmation

Failure means you had the right idea but
maybe not yet all the tools you needed.

NOVEMBER

Do something you truly love,
and your vision will pull you along.

Birthday Affirmation

♏

Talent determines what you can do, but your attitude determines how well you do it.

NOVEMBER

Stay true to your authentic self and never let anyone distract you from this.

Birthday Affirmation

SCORPIO

Daily Affirmation

A leader focuses on solutions,
not problems.

NOVEMBER

12

Let your choices reflect your hopes
and not your fears.

Birthday Affirmation

♏

Daily Affirmation

To accomplish your goals, go as far
as you can and then take another step.

NOVEMBER

13

Every day is a new beginning,
start afresh regardless of what is in the past.

Birthday Affirmation

SCORPIO

Make your internal life your focus and
everything you need will come your way.

NOVEMBER

Breathe, trust, let go and embrace
what happens next.

Birthday Affirmation

♏

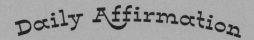

Daily Affirmation

Don't run back to the old ways just because
they are familiar and so feel safe.

NOVEMBER

Never assume that what's right
for you is right for everyone else.

Birthday Affirmation

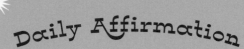

Daily Affirmation

Day by day, every little thing is adding
up to take you somewhere wonderful.

NOVEMBER

Plant the seeds of commitment to your goals
and watch them grow.

Birthday Affirmation

♏

What goes around comes around,
but sometimes we have to wait our turn.

NOVEMBER

Nourish those friendships
that nourish you.

SCORPIO

337

Daily Affirmation

Difficult roads often lead
to beautiful destinations.

NOVEMBER

18

Your mind is powerful, so fill it with positive
thoughts to harness that power.

Birthday Affirmation

♏

You will become successful
the very second you decide to be.

NOVEMBER

Each day you become a little more yourself
than you were the day before.

Birthday Affirmation

SCORPIO

Daily Affirmation

Act as if what you are doing makes a difference
and before you know it, it does.

NOVEMBER

20

The more grateful you are,
the more present you become.

Birthday Affirmation

♏

Daily Affirmation

Tell yourself that no matter how hard
it is or gets, you are going to make it.

NOVEMBER

21

You are braver than you believe, stronger
than you seem and smarter than you think.

Birthday Affirmation

SCORPIO

Daily Affirmation

Push yourself – don't wait
for someone else to do it.

NOVEMBER

22

Don't allow anyone to dull
your soul's sparkle.

Birthday Affirmation

♐

If anyone expresses doubts about how far you
can go, go so far you can't hear them.

NOVEMBER

23

You will always pass failure
on your way to success.

Birthday Affirmation

Daily Affirmation

Sometimes, a moment has to become
a memory for us to truly understand its value.

NOVEMBER

24

Where there is real love
there is always inspiration.

Birthday Affirmation

♐

Daily Affirmation

If you think what you've always thought,
you'll get what you always got.

NOVEMBER

25

If your dreams don't thrill you,
you need to dream bigger.

Birthday Affirmation

Daily Affirmation

If you want to succeed, focus on your goals,
not the blocks in your way.

NOVEMBER

26

Fearlessness is like a muscle: the more
you use it the stronger it grows.

Birthday Affirmation

↗

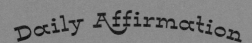

Daily Affirmation

If you don't ever take a risk, you
end up risking everything.

NOVEMBER

27

Learning to master yourself
is where your real power lies.

Birthday Affirmation

When you get tired, learn to rest
properly instead of just quitting.

NOVEMBER

28

You can't become exactly who you want
to become by staying just as you are.

Birthday Affirmation

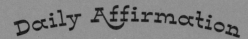

Daily Affirmation

You may be stuck with the beginning, but you can always change the ending.

NOVEMBER

29

Life doesn't come with a remote,
you need to get up and change the channel.

Birthday Affirmation

Daily Affirmation

You get what you work hard for,
not what you just wish for.

NOVEMBER

30

Eyes forward. Mind focused.
Heart ready. Game on.

Birthday Affirmation

♐

Work as hard as you can in silence
and let your success be your noise.

DECEMBER

You are the single greatest project you
will ever have the privilege to work on.

Birthday Affirmation

Daily Affirmation

Your path may be different, but that
does not mean you will get lost.

DECEMBER

02

Remember just how far
you have come.

Birthday Affirmation

Daily Affirmation

Some things will come along that break
your heart but fix your vision.

DECEMBER

03

Nobody has yet found an elevator to success,
so you'll need to take the stairs.

Birthday Affirmation

Bravery is not an absence of fear but finding
the courage to push on through it.

DECEMBER

It is not the mountain you need
to conquer; it is your own fears.

Daily Affirmation

Don't be busy,
be productive.

DECEMBER

05

Don't waste any more precious time
waiting for tomorrow.

Birthday Affirmation

SAGITTARIUS

Daily Affirmation

Life is a circle, so if you are facing hard times, know that good times are on their way.

DECEMBER

Your success is built on all those small efforts you repeat, day in and day out.

Birthday Affirmation

You'll never know how strong you are until being strong is your only option.

DECEMBER

Even if you are on the right track, you'll get run over if you just sit there.

Birthday Affirmation

Daily Affirmation

Never let one small stumble on the road signal
the end of the journey – it's not.

DECEMBER

Walk barefoot. Listen to the wind.
Drink in sunlight. Be magical.

Birthday Affirmation

♐

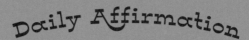

Daily Affirmation

Discipline is the bridge between our goals
and their accomplishment.

DECEMBER

Power is not gifted to us –
we have to decide to take it.

Birthday Affirmation

Falling down is an accident, but
staying down is a choice.

DECEMBER

10

Seize the day, and every one
that follows this one.

Daily Affirmation

We rise higher and highest
by lifting others.

DECEMBER

A tiger doesn't lose sleep worrying about
the opinion of a sheep.

Birthday Affirmation

SAGITTARIUS

361

Don't wake with regrets about yesterday,
focus on what you will do today.

DECEMBER

12

You were made from love, to be loved
and to spread and share the love.

Birthday Affirmation

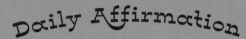

Daily Affirmation

Don't fear success and inadvertently
give up before achieving it.

DECEMBER

13

Little things make big
and memorable days.

Birthday Affirmation

Forget the mistake but remember the lesson.

DECEMBER

One day or day one – it's your choice.

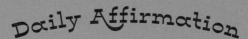

Daily Affirmation

The goal is not to live forever
but to create something that will.

DECEMBER

15

You were born an original, so don't die a copy.

Birthday Affirmation

Daily Affirmation

If you want a seat at the table, try to show up
with something special.

DECEMBER

Design a life for yourself that
you'll feel inspired to be living.

Birthday Affirmation

Daily Affirmation

If life says put something down it's because
there's something better to pick up.

DECEMBER

Do what you know is right,
not what feels easy.

Birthday Affirmation

Daily Affirmation

If you think you are too small to make a difference, remember that several small actions add up to big changes.

DECEMBER

Open your heart to the world's wonders, it is its own reward.

Birthday Affirmation

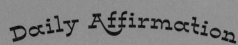
Daily Affirmation

Don't compare your life to anyone else's;
their journey is not the same as yours.

DECEMBER

19

Be your own best friend,
every day.

Birthday Affirmation

Daily Affirmation

Don't use the 'no time' excuse, you have the
same hours in a day as all the greats.

DECEMBER

20

Write a letter to your future and tell it,
'I'm ready.'

Birthday Affirmation

♐

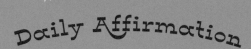

Daily Affirmation

Look for opportunity
in the middle of every difficulty.

DECEMBER

21

Just as water always finds its own level,
whatever is meant to be will be.

Birthday Affirmation

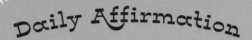

Daily Affirmation

Growing as a person isn't always comfortable,
but it's always within your scope.

DECEMBER

22

How you choose to show up will determine
what, in turn, shows up for you.

Birthday Affirmation

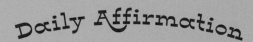
Your talent will open the door, but your application of it will keep you in the room.

DECEMBER

23

Shift your perspective if necessary to ensure there's always an element of fun in life.

Birthday Affirmation

Daily Affirmation

If it lowers your energy in any way,
reconsider if it's right for you.

DECEMBER

24

Choose to focus on what's positive,
and see the difference it makes.

Birthday Affirmation

Daily Affirmation

Your self-worth is your business
and should not be decided by others.

DECEMBER

25

What you want in life will come
when your heart is ready to carry it.

Birthday Affirmation

Daily Affirmation

Those people who make you feel you're too
much? They're not your people.

DECEMBER

26

Life can be tough, yes; but if necessary,
so can you.

Birthday Affirmation

Worrying does not take away your troubles,
it just takes away your peace.

DECEMBER

27

Make yourself a priority
in your own life.

Birthday Affirmation

CAPRICORN

Daily Affirmation

Be quick to listen
but slow to speak.

DECEMBER

28

If you don't know what's hampering your
dreams, look beyond the obvious.

Birthday Affirmation

Don't linger too long anywhere
that hurts your heart.

DECEMBER

29

Relinquish control and look
for the hidden gifts that may result.

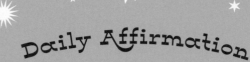

Daily Affirmation

Forget how you think it should
be and accept how it is.

DECEMBER

30

Be smart enough to walk through
any door that opens to you.

Birthday Affirmation

Daily Affirmation

Whatever you lose will come back in a new form, so don't waste time on regret.

DECEMBER

31

A diamond is just a lump of coal that flourished under pressure.

Birthday Affirmation

ABOUT THE AUTHOR

Stella Andromeda has been studying astrology for over 30 years, believing that a knowledge of the constellations of the skies and their potential for psychological interpretation can be a useful tool. This extension of her study into book form makes modern insights about the ancient wisdom of the stars easily accessible, sharing her passion that reflection and self-knowledge only empower us in life. With her sun in Taurus, Aquarius ascendant and Moon in Cancer, she utilises earth, air and water to inspire her own astrological journey.

Stella Andromeda is also author of the 12 *Seeing Stars* astrological sun sign series, along with *Love Match*, *Cat Astrology*, *Dog Astrology* and *AstroBirthdays*, all published by Hardie Grant.

ACKNOWLEDGEMENTS

Thanks as ever are due to the hardworking team at Hardie Grant, Kate Burkett and Chelsea Edwards, for their continued commitment to this astrological series, and also to Kate Pollard, its original publisher. Special thanks are also due to Evi O. for their lovely design and illustrations.

Published in 2022 by Hardie Grant Books,
an imprint of Hardie Grant Publishing

Hardie Grant Books (London)
5th & 6th Floors
52–54 Southwark Street
London, SE1 1UN

Hardie Grant Books (Melbourne)
Building 1, 658 Church Street
Richmond, Victoria 3121
hardiegrantbooks.com

British Library Cataloguing-in-Publication Data. A catalogue record for this book
is available from the British Library.

ISBN: 978-1-78488-535-9

10 9 8 7 6 5 4 3 2 1

Publishing Director: Kajal Mistry
Commissioning Editor: Kate Burkett
Senior Editor: Chelsea Edwards
Art Direction and Illustrations: Evi O. Studio | Wilson Leung, Katherine Zhang & Emi Chiba
Production Controller: Sabeena Atchia

Colour reproduction by p2d
Printed and bound in China by Leo Paper Products Ltd